11 Plus Workbook Answers

Author: Christine R. Draper and Phillip R. Draper

CW01657637

This book contains the Answers for the following workbooks:

11 Plus Non-Verbal Reasoning by Christine R. and Phillip R. Draper ISBN: 978-1-909986-77-0

11 Plus Maths by Christine R. Draper ISBN: 978-1-909986-75-6

11 Plus Verbal & English by Christine R. Draper. ISBN: 978-1-909986-76-3

11 Plus Verbal Reasoning (GL-style) by Christine R Draper. ISBN: 978-1-909986-48-0

These answers are also available at: http://www.achieve2day.co.uk/workbooks

Published: achieve2day, Slough, 2016

ISBN: 9781909986336

Contents

Non-Verbal Reasoning Answers

Chapter 1

Practice questions:

1. B,E,F
2. A,B,D,E
3. B & F
4. C, E, G

Exercise 1.

1. C (Curved)
2. C (Not regular)
3. A (No straight sides)
4. E (5 Sides not 6)
5. D (3 circles, not 2, no square)
6. D (Top left shape not the same as outside shape)
7. B (7 sides)
8. E (Series: circle – square – circle, black grey white)
9. A (Inside shape becomes outside shape as the series progresses)
10. C (End flat, point to the left)

Chapter 2.

Practice questions:

1. B,E
2. A,B,D
3. B,D
4. B,E

Exercise 2:

1. D (No straight lines)
2. D (Different thicknesses of vertical lines)
3. C (Black vertical line)
4. A (3 straight lines)
5. B (Dashed line not dotted)
6. D (Small dots become straight grey lines, big dots become dark curves)
7. C (Black lines go through all of the dots)
8. A (Same shape, white fill becomes right slant shading)
9. C (One more side added, same line type)
10. C (Outside shape plus one side, dotted lines to dashed, inside shape minus one side)

Chapter 3:

Practice questions:

1. C
2. B
3. E
4. D

Exercise 3:

1. D (Same arrow head)
2. B (Arrow points towards the circle)
3. D (Arrow points anti-clockwise, square is at bottom, triangle at top)
4. D (Arrow is straight and pointed left)
5. A (Asterisk and arrow in same column(vertical))
6. C (Arrow points towards a side, not a corner)
7. E (Odd number of arrowheads)
8. C (No enclosed shape on end of arrow)
9. A (First arrow turns 90 degrees anticlockwise to form second arrow, all others turn clockwise)
10. E (Arrow point points towards the middle of the square, all others point towards a side)

Exercise 4:

1. B (Centre shape is black which has one less side than the outside shape, line fills)
2. C (Rotated shape white circle)
3. D (Left shapes are white and linked, all 4 shapes around the circle are the same)
4. C (2 pairs of curved lines)
5. A (Four sides, lines form corners, white circle in centre)
6. B (Number of dots increases by one, repeating series: circle, triangle, square (repeating pattern)
7. D (Arrows alternate pointing left right, number of arrows increases by one)
8. B (Arrow head type repeats. Arrow heads alternate pointing upwards and downwards. Background shading alternates: horizontal and vertical lined fill)
9. A (Alternate dotted and horizontal lined fill, the shape adds a side each time, background colour fill repeats: black, grey, white)
10. D (Black filled circle changes position (one half side) anticlockwise, number of circle in the centre increases by one)

Exercise 5:

1. B (Number of sides increases by one, number of circles increase by one)
2. B (Triangles alternate 2/1, circles alternate 4/3, squares increase by one)
3. C (Series adds one more oval (petal) clockwise)
4. E (Asterisks in series: 1, 2, 3, 2, 1. sides have the series: 6,5,4,5,6)
5. E (Lines at top decrease by 1 line, removing alternatively in a left right pattern. Horizontal line at the bottom (base) alternates)
6. C (Only one with two rectangles)
7. E (The middle shape has two less side than the outside shape, all the others only have one less side)
8. A (The number of the smallest lines does not equal the number of "main" branches)
9. D (The number of circles is not the same as the number of lines at the top of the shape)
10. D (The shape has seven sides not six)

Chapter 6:

1. C (Reflected vertically)
2. C (Reflected horizontally)
3. A (Reflected horizontally)
4. B (Reflected vertically)
5. B (Reflected horizontally)
6. E (Reflected horizontally)
7. D (Reflected vertically)
8. C (Reflected horizontally)
9. D (Reflected horizontally)
10. A (Reflected horizontally)

Chapter 7:

Practice questions:

1. A
2. B
3. B, D
4. A,D

Exercise 7:

1. B
2. A
3. C
4. D
5. B
6. A
7. C
8. B
9. B
10. E

Exercise 8:

1. C (Shape rotates 45° clockwise, alternating horizontal/white)
2. B (Circle moves around the square anticlockwise, grey square moves clockwise half a side, black square moves clockwise half a side)
3. A (Fills rotate 45°, shapes repeat: diamond, circle, square)
4. E (Black circle rotates clockwise, white circle rotates clockwise around the outside)
5. D (Line rotates 45° clockwise, arrow heads repeat: thin barbed, equilateral, large barbed)
6. B (Shapes rotate 90° clockwise, fills swap)
7. D (Not a rotation)
8. B (Fill not rotated with shape)
9. E (Not a rotation)
10. C (Not a rotation)

Exercise 9:

1. B (Shape becomes bigger)
2. B (Shape is squashed)
3. C (Shape is stretched vertically and two lines added)
4. C (Top shape gets bigger, bottom shape remains the same)
5. E (Top shape gets smaller, bottom shape remains the same)
6. D (Smaller square)
7. E (Inside shape not squashed)
8. B (Two shapes the same, other shapes stretched not squashed)
9. E (Shape stretched)
10. B (Arrow is smaller)

Exercise 10:

1. A (Overlay not a link)
2. C (Big shape does not go all the way across the other large shape)
3. D (Oval linked to triangle not the square)
4. D (Rectangle is grey, can see all of rectangle)
5. C (Overlap forms a four sided shape, not a three sided shape)
6. D (Cannot see all of grey circle)
7. D (Overlap forms the same shape as the larger shapes)
8. C (Three shapes the same, one overlay, two links)
9. D (Rectangle partially through the long "leg" of the "T" shape)
10. A (Shapes are different, four sided overlap)

Exercise 11:

1. A (Shapes alternate left to right, all shapes move: bottom, middle, top)
2. D (Circle moves clockwise, triangle alternates top to bottom, square moves clockwise, not A as triangle does NOT change orientation)
3. D (Triangles are removed in a clockwise direction, circles are added anti-clockwise, colour alternates: black / white)
4. E (arrow alternates up / down, arrow location alternates left-right, fills repeat: top, top, middle, middle, bottom, bottom)
5. C (grey stays in top right corner, white circle moves clockwise, grey covers white if in same space)
6. SR (First letter is the position of the triangle (left, right or middle), second letter is the fill colour of circle (white, black or grey))
7. FB (First letter corner pentagon is pointing to, second letter is fill colour of the pentagon)
8. GB (First letter is vertical position of the chevron, second letter is the horizontal position of the chevron (Colour in this case is irrelevant, as it doesn't fit a logical pattern of either letter))
9. SV (First letter is the direction of the triangles, second letter is the horizontal position of the letter)
10. QS (First letter is the outside shape, second letter is the shading (direction) of the inside shape)

Exercise 12:

1. B (No vertical symmetry)
2. E (Cross-hatched shading not lines)
3. E (Not a rotation)
4. C (Arrow does not start from the black circle)
5. E (Not concave at one end of the shape)
6. A (No right angles)
7. D (Three circles not two, no circle in top left)
8. D (Doesn't have the same number of little "branches" as main "branches" 2 instead of 3)
9. B (Curved outer shape)
10. C (Only shape with a line of vertical or horizontal symmetry)

Exercise 13:

1. C (Sides of both shapes add up to 10 total sides)
2. B (Overlap we see all of the bottom shape, the shapes are diagonal from top right to bottom left)
3. A (Circle is at the top of the shape, bottom left shape is a smaller version of the outside shape)
4. D (Middle of the three internal lines is a line of symmetry, shape has straight sides)
5. B (The overlap makes same shape as the larger shapes)
6. A (Twice as many black shapes as white shapes)
7. D (Vertical symmetry)
8. B (Bottom shape is a 180° rotation of the top shape)

9. C (Outside shape has a solid line, the inside shapes are the same as the outside shape, all shapes have the same orientation)
10. D (Same shape rotated)

Exercise 14:

1. D (First letter is shape, second letter is colour)
2. A (First letter outside shape and top shape the same, second letter is outside shape and bottom shape the same)
3. A (First letter is straight / curved lines, second letter is fill colour)
4. C (First letter is the direction, second is arrowhead type)
5. D (First letter is shape, second is fill direction, third is line type (heavy/light))
6. B (First letter is number of black shapes, second is number of white shapes, third is whether the white shapes are on the left or right side)
7. C (First letter is circle on corner or side of shape, second number of sides, third letter is fill colour of circle)
8. E (First letter top left shaded, second bottom left shaded, third is colour of shading)
9. D (First letter is number of lines on arrow shaft, second is the direction of the arrow, third is position of the lines on the arrow shaft)
10. D (First letter is curved/straight base, second is straight/curved top, third is right/left orientation of dots (please note that dot colour is not used)

Exercise 15:

1. C (Vertically: outside shape reflects – lines swap)
2. C (Vertically: Shape reflects, colours swap (black/grey))
3. E (Horizontally: shape rotates 180°, line in middle changes type)
4. C (Horizontally: Outside shape filled grey, the two inside shapes swap positions)
5. B (Horizontally: curved line is reflection, shape increases by two sides)
6. A (Each row has one of each colour/shape)
7. B (Each row has a small medium and long arrow, arrows rotate clockwise)
8. D (Each column has one of each shape, each shape type has one of each of the fill types)
9. E (Arrowheads alternately point up or down, third column is squares, each row has the same number of shapes, colours alternate through the rows)
10. A (Horizontally: two outside squares combine to make the middle shape)

Exercise 16:

1. B (Number of sides increases then decreases, shapes with same number of sides are different, opposite shapes are shaded the same)
2. B (Starting from centre top: dot added clockwise)
3. C (Rotates anti clockwise 90°, size increases)
4. D (Arrows alternate direction inwards/outwards, circles are opposite ends to the arrowheads, number of circles is the same as the opposite segment)
5. A (1/4 of a circle added, circle swaps direction)
6. E (rotates 45°, opposite segments are the same)
7. D (Clockwise from top - large circle repeats: black, grey, white, large semi-circles alternate black / grey, small black semi-circle rotates clockwise)

8. B (pattern adds one grey(missing a segment) then adds one black in the empty segments, the shading is added in a clockwise fashion)
9. A (Arrow points to corner of hexagon rotating in clockwise direction, square/circle alternates)
10. E (From top shapes repeat: circle, square, triangle; shading rotates)

Exercise 17

1. E (Grouped circles alternate left/right slant, complete circle visible repeats: bottom middle top)
2. B (Repeats: triangle, circle, square; shading alternates)
3. A (Shield/circle shapes alternate, horizontal lines in shield decrease by one, shapes and lines within shield alternate top/bottom, shapes within shield alternate circles/squares)
4. D (Rotates 90° clockwise)
5. D (Rotates 90° clockwise, colours of small rectangles swap)
6. B (Base shape alternates, one "branch" added each time on alternate side, added line is the bottom 'branch')
7. A (Number of crosses, 3,2,2,1,1. circles: 2,2,1,1,0. triangles 0,1,2,3,4)
8. A (Shapes have one less side, shading rotates 45°clockwise, all have flat bases)
9. C (one less line each time, arrowhead moves 90° anticlockwise, origin point is top left, arrowhead alternate barbed/equilateral)
10. E (White circle rotates one line anticlockwise, black circle rotates one line clockwise)

Exercise 18

1. F (Working from left to right we see that the crosses are decreasing by one each time, boxes increase by one each time, while boxes alternate sides, crosses do not)
2. C (As above)
3. B (Cross repeats: none, medium, large, medium, none)
4. D (As above)
5. A (Circles alternate black / white, circles move down from each alternate side)
6. E (As above)
7. E (The large shape in each frame becomes the smaller shape in the next frame rotating 180°)
8. A (As above)
9. D (Dashed line become solid, dashed line added anti-clockwise to form next section of hexagon, circle fills repeat horizontal lines, black, white)
10. E (As above)

Exercise 19:

1. C (Vertical reflection, colour change between grey and black)
2. B (Rotates 45°anticlockwise)
3. C (Inside shape vertical reflection of outside shape, outside shape rotates 180°)
4. A (Outside shape rotates 90° and becomes the inside shape; inside shape becomes the outside shape, and the insides shapes' shading becomes the shading between the inside and next layer. Inside shapes' shading becomes white)
5. E (Inside shape rotates 180°, outside shading 90°, inside shading rotates 90°
6. B (Shapes move anticlockwise, black/white background alternates, shading stays the same for each position)
7. D (Two shapes the same as original added on right, the two shapes are medium and small copies of original, medium added to bottom right, small top right, all link to each other shape in same orientation as original)
8. E (Top right quarter of shape removed, fill swaps)
9. D (Overlap becomes outside shape, shape on left becomes inside shape)
10. C (Line added to bottom, top small shape repeated, bottom little shape repeated, black circle disappears, all small shapes are bounded on two sides by line

Exercise 20:

1. C
2. B
3. A
4. D
5. C
6. B
7. D
8. B
9. D
10. C

Exercise 21:

1. A (B - top, C - front, D - side)
2. C (A - top, B - side, D - front)
3. D (A - top, B - front, C - side)
4. C (A - top, B - side, D - front)
5. D (A - top, V - front, C - side)
6. D (A - front, B - side, C - top)
7. C (top)
8. B (top)
9. C (top)
10. D (top)

Exercise 22:

1. D
2. A
3. D
4. A
5. C
6. A
7. E
8. D
9. C
10. B

Exercise 23:

1. C
2. D
3. A
4. B
5. C
6. A
7. B
8. D
9. C
10. A

Exercise 24

1. D
2. B
3. B
4. D
5. D
6. C
7. A
8. C
9. B
10. A

Exercise 25:

1. B
2. D
3. B
4. D
5. D
6. C
7. D
8. E
9. B
10. B

Exercise 26:

1. D
2. C
3. C
4. C
5. B
6. D
7. D
8. A
9. B
10. D

Exercise 27

1. A
2. B
3. D
4. C
5. D
6. A
7. D
8. C
9. C
10. A

Exercise 28:

1. A
2. D
3. A
4. B
5. D
6. B
7. C
8. B
9. C
10. B

Exercise 29:

1. B
2. B
3. A
4. D
5. C
6. B
7. A
8. B
9. C
10. C

Exercise 30:

1. D
2. B
3. C
4. B
5. A
6. D
7. D
8. C
9. C
10. B

Numerical Reasoning Answers

Exercise 1.1a

1. 11
2. 58
3. 301
4. 42 006
5. 362 000
6. 1 003 022
7. 5 060 045
8. 0.2
9. 0.09
10. 7.2

Exercise 1.1b

1. twenty seven
2. thirteen
3. four hundred and thirty two
4. three thousand five hundred and two
5. twenty six thousand and twenty three
6. one hundred and three thousand and four
7. one million six hundred and fifty four thousand
8. two million, two thousand and two
9. one tenth, or zero point one
10. zero point zero zero seven or seven thousandths

Exercise 1.1c

1. $\frac{1}{10}$
2. $\frac{9}{100}$
3. 6
4. $\frac{2}{10}$
5. $\frac{8}{100}$
6. $\frac{2}{1000}$
7. $\frac{5}{10}+\frac{6}{100}$
8. $\frac{56}{100}$
9. $\frac{107}{1000}$
10. $\frac{173}{1000}$

Exercise 1.2

1. 6201 6032 5721 3222 521 11
2. 9067 5781 2001 1002 999 345
3. 1.3 1.001 0.2 0.04 0.01 0.009
4. 326
5. 101
6. 0.3
7. 34 < 52
8. 803 > 789
9. 0.34 > 0.211
10. 0.02 > 0.001

Exercise 1.3

1. -3
2. -12
3. -6
4. -3
5. -2 -1 0 1 2
6. -4°C < -2°C
7. -16°C > -17°C
8. -20°C < 20°C
9. 12°
10. -15°C

Exercise 1.4

1. 60
2. 40
3. 470
4. 300
5. 37
6. 49
7. 56
8. 40
9. 38.72
10. 49.38

Exercise 1.5

1. 5
2. 8
3. 502 062
4. 392
5. 0.0009
6. -30
7. -7
8. 70
9. 190
10. 3.88

Exercise 2.1

1. 899
2. 1045
3. 1314
4. 1658
5. 2000
6. 187
7. 93
8. 570
9. 45
10. 1130

Exercise 2.2

1. 1.86
2. 4.01
3. 8.17
4. 9.44
5. 12.02
6. 9.37
7. £19.11
8. 146.9cm
9.

```
   [9][1] 7
 -  8  3 [3]
 -----------
       8  4

    3 [4] 4
 +  9  4  3
 -----------
 1 [2] 8 [7]
```

10.

```
    8 [8] 7
 +  8  9 [7]
 -----------
 1 [7] 8  4
```

Exercise 2.3

1. 612
2. 1152
3. 979
4. 992
5. 2673
6. 936
7. £42
8. 473
9. 244
10. 91

Exercise 2.4

1. 1.21
2. 1.75
3. 0.88
4. 0.63
5. 5.2cm
6. 0.4kg
7. 1.3kg
8. 1.9 miles
9.

```
   [9][1] 7
 -  8  3 [3]
 -----------
       8  4
```

10.

```
   [9] 4  2
 -  8  3 [8]
 -----------
    1 [0] 4
```

Exercise 2.5

1. 396
2. 1054
3. 472
4. 29.78
5. 32
6. 52.6cm
7. 299
8. £1.45
9. 29
10. 141

Exercise 3.1

1. 6200
2. 3420
3. 480
4. 960
5. 324.78
6. 56.71
7. 0.462
8. 3230
9. 0.0045
10. 380

Exercise 3.2

1. 171
2. 672
3. 17 108
4. 208
5. 153
6. 896
7. 832
8. 272
9. 3450
10. 391cm^2

Exercise 3.3

1. 197
2. 54
3. 194 r 1
4. 1072
5. 963 r 2
6. 976 r 2
7. 118.8
8. 183.25
9. 125.7
10. 54.4

Exercise 3.4

1. 524
2. 654
3. 369
4. 63
5. 63.25
6. 45.5
7. 37.8
8. 216.1
9. 357.7
10. 392.3

Exercise 3.5

1. £282
2. 129
3. £216
4. 4250
5. 489 litres
6. 8
7. 168 miles
8. 720
9. 15
10. 3

Puzzle Page 1

1. 1012
2. 1258
3. 4783
4. 1120
5. 1200
6. 4683
7. 0.42
8. 113.4
9. 200
10. 112.4
11. 14
12. -200
13. 4.2

They improve di-vision

Exercise 4.1

14. -4
15. 4
16. -27
17. 14
18. -8
19. 16
20. -32
21. 18
22. 1
23. 9

Exercise 4.2

1. 17
2. 11
3. 20
4. 15
5. 10
6. 17
7. 10
8. 10
9. 30
10. 20

Exercise 4.3

1. 71
2. 11
3. £71.20
4. 33
5. 40
6. £20 000
7. 6
8. 36
9. 20 minutes
10. 38 pages

Exercise 4.4

1. 6
2. 40
3. 2
4. 7
5. 3
6. 7
7. 4
8. 3
9. 8
10. 9

Exercise 4.5

1. -7°C
2. 7°C
3. £50
4. 11
5. 37
6. 6
7. 145 cm
8. 64
9. 6
10. 8

Exercise 5.1

1. 1, 5
2. 1, 2, 5, 10
3. 1, 2, 11, 22
4. 1, 2, 3, 4, 6, 8, 12, 24
5. 1, 7
6. 1, 2, 3, 4, 6, 9, 12, 18, 36
7. 1, 2, 4, 7, 14, 28
8. 1, 3, 5, 15
9. 1, 2, 4, 8, 16
10. 1, 2, 4, 8, 16, 32, 64

Exercise 5.2

1. 12, 24, 36, 48, 60, 72
2. 4, 8, 12, 16, 20, 24
3. 7, 14, 21, 28, 35, 42
4. 15, 30, 45, 60, 75, 90
5. 20, 40, 60, 80, 100, 120
6. 16, 32, 48, 64, 80, 96
7. 17, 34, 51, 68
8. 25, 50, 75, 100
9. 14, 28, 42, 56
10. 36. 72, 108, 144

Exercise 5.3

1. P
2. R
3. R
4. P
5. P
6. R
7. 2 x 3 x 5 x 7
8. 2 x 2 x 2 x 3 (or 2^3 x 3)
9. 2 x 2 x 2 x 3 x 3 x 5 (or 2^3 x 3^2 x 5)
10. 5 x 5 x 7 (or 5^2 x 7)

Exercise 5.4

1. 9
2. 81
3. 144
4. 225
5. 169
6. 10 000
7. 3
8. 8
9. 11
10. 7

Exercise 5.5

1. 1, 3, 9, 27
2. 1, 2, 3, 6, 9, 18
3. 1, 2, 3, 4, 6, 8, 12, 16, 24, 48
4. 8, 16, 24, 32
5. 6, 12, 18, 24
6. 13, 26, 39, 52
7. Prime
8. 4^2
9. 6
10. 625

Exercise 6.1

1. 6
2. 140
3. 1.4
4. 27
5. 2.2
6. 650
7. 2.6
8. 33
9. 4.3
10. 4.75 or $4\frac{3}{4}$

Exercise 6.2

1. 37 x 37 x 37 x 37
2. 58 x 58 x 58 x 58 x 58
3. 19 x 19 x 19
4. 8
5. 1
6. 64
7. 32
8. 243
9. 125
10. 1 000 000

Exercise 6.3

1. 3
2. 3
3. 5
4. 6
5. 1
6. 6
7. 20
8. 8
9. 7
10. 6 baskets
    3 oranges
    4 pears
    6 bananas

Exercise 6.4

1. 18
2. 63
3. 25
4. 36
5. 36
6. 24
7. 24
8. 24
9. 5
10. 60

Exercise 6.5

1. 105
2. 6.5
3. 0.56
4. 256
5. 81
6. 13
7. 18
8. 30
9. 36”
10. 6

Exercise 7.1

1. shaded: $\frac{1}{6}$ unshaded: $\frac{5}{6}$
2. shaded: $\frac{5}{6}$ unshaded: $\frac{1}{6}$
3. shaded: $\frac{5}{16}$ unshaded: $\frac{11}{16}$
4. shaded: $\frac{2}{3}$ unshaded: $\frac{1}{3}$
5. shaded: $\frac{15}{16}$ unshaded: $\frac{1}{16}$
6. $7 \div 9$
7. $11 \div 17$
8. $2 \div 3$
9. $5 \div 7$
10. $5 \div 12$

Exercise 7.2a

1. 15
2. 9
3. 2
4. 3, 28
5. 15, 48
6. 7
7. 19
8. 40, 100
9. 132, 4
10. 25, 180

Exercise 7.2b

1. 10
2. 27
3. 4
4. 7
5. 18
6. 42
7. 56
8. 160
9. 33
10. 30

Exercise 7.3

1. $\frac{2}{3}$
2. $\frac{1}{3}$
3. $\frac{2}{3}$
4. $\frac{1}{3}$
5. $\frac{3}{7}$
6. $\frac{7}{12}$
7. $\frac{2}{9}$
8. $\frac{1}{4}$
9. $\frac{7}{10}$
10. $\frac{2}{3}$

Exercise 7.4a

1. Improper $\frac{9}{8}$ mixed $1\frac{1}{8}$
2. Improper $\frac{9}{5}$ mixed $1\frac{4}{5}$
3. Improper $\frac{29}{12}$ mixed $2\frac{5}{12}$
4. Improper $\frac{28}{12}$ or $\frac{7}{3}$ mixed $2\frac{1}{3}$
5. Improper $\frac{21}{11}$ mixed $1\frac{10}{11}$
6. Improper $\frac{14}{6}$ or $\frac{7}{3}$ mixed $2\frac{1}{3}$
7. Improper $\frac{11}{8}$ mixed $1\frac{3}{8}$
8. Improper $\frac{14}{5}$ mixed $2\frac{4}{5}$
9. Improper $\frac{24}{10}$ or $\frac{12}{5}$ mixed $2\frac{2}{5}$
10. Improper $\frac{15}{9}$ or $\frac{5}{3}$ mixed $1\frac{2}{3}$

Exercise 7.4b

1. $2\frac{1}{4}$
2. $5\frac{2}{5}$
3. $1\frac{5}{9}$
4. $1\frac{3}{8}$
5. $2\frac{1}{5}$
6. $\frac{17}{5}$
7. $\frac{24}{13}$
8. $\frac{79}{20}$
9. $\frac{60}{7}$
10. $\frac{95}{6}$

Exercise 7.5

1. 9
2. 36
3. 60
4. 12
5. 55
6. $\frac{21}{30}$ and $\frac{10}{30}$
7. $\frac{3}{9}$ and $\frac{4}{9}$
8. $\frac{50}{60}$ and $\frac{3}{60}$
9. $\frac{15}{24}$ and $\frac{10}{24}$
10. $\frac{14}{54}$ and $\frac{45}{54}$

Exercise 8.1

1. $\frac{6}{7}$
2. $\frac{5}{11}$
3. $\frac{2}{3}$
4. $1\frac{1}{6}$
5. 1
6. $\frac{17}{20}$
7. $\frac{31}{42}$
8. $\frac{7}{18}$
9. $1\frac{11}{20}$
10. $1\frac{17}{36}$

Exercise 8.2

1. $\frac{2}{7}$
2. $\frac{7}{11}$
3. $\frac{1}{3}$
4. $\frac{1}{6}$
5. $\frac{7}{20}$
6. $\frac{1}{24}$
7. $\frac{1}{9}$
8. $\frac{1}{18}$
9. $\frac{7}{20}$
10. $\frac{11}{36}$

Exercise 8.3

1. $\frac{5}{24}$
2. $\frac{8}{25}$
3. $\frac{14}{33}$
4. $\frac{12}{23}$
5. $1\frac{1}{2}$
6. $\frac{1}{6}$
7. $\frac{1}{4}$
8. $\frac{3}{5}$
9. $\frac{3}{8}$
10. $\frac{11}{27}$

Exercise 8.4

1. $\frac{1}{2}$
2. $1\frac{1}{3}$
3. $1\frac{1}{2}$
4. $1\frac{1}{2}$
5. $1\frac{1}{2}$
6. $\frac{1}{2}$
7. $\frac{1}{2}$
8. $\frac{2}{3}$
9. $\frac{11}{24}$
10. $\frac{3}{20}$

Exercise 8.5a

1. $3\frac{5}{6}$
2. 6
3. $7\frac{9}{11}$
4. $6\frac{2}{5}$
5. $10\frac{7}{10}$
6. $5\frac{2}{3}$
7. $4\frac{5}{9}$
8. $1\frac{6}{7}$
9. $3\frac{11}{24}$
10. $\frac{14}{15}$

Exercise 8.5b

1. $2\frac{1}{6}$
2. $7\frac{1}{2}$
3. 20
4. 18
5. $21\frac{1}{3}$
6. 6
7. 2
8. $\frac{1}{4}$
9. $\frac{21}{104}$
10. $\frac{1}{3}$

Exercise 9.1

1. $\frac{5}{8}$
2. $\frac{1}{8}$
3. $\frac{5}{7}$
4. $\frac{2}{5}$
5. $\frac{3}{4}$
6. $\frac{3}{5}$
7. $\frac{7}{9}$
8. $\frac{4}{7}$
9. $\frac{3}{11}$
10. $\frac{7}{12}$

Exercise 9.2

1. 28
2. 12
3. 400
4. 45
5. 368
6. 360
7. 12
8. 240
9. 28
10. 24

Exercise 9.3

1. 35
2. 81
3. 56
4. 96
5. 108
6. 200
7. 35
8. 42
9. 18
10. 54

Exercise 9.4

1. 60
2. 14
3. 40
4. 40
5. 18
6. 16
7. 180
8. 15
9. 54
10. £13.50

Exercise 10.1

1. 17%
2. 25%
3. 56%
4. 3%
5. 49%
6. 9%
7. 89%
8. 312%
9. 777%
10. 503%

Exercise 10.2

1. $\frac{37}{100}$
2. $\frac{23}{100}$
3. $\frac{3}{5}$
4. $\frac{1}{4}$
5. $\frac{1}{2}$
6. $\frac{6}{25}$
7. $\frac{7}{20}$
8. $\frac{1}{20}$
9. $5\frac{4}{5}$
10. $1\frac{18}{25}$

Exercise 10.3

1. 70%
2. 60%
3. 24%
4. 55%
5. 26%
6. 95%
7. 92%
8. 160%
9. 140%
10. 205%

Exercise 10.4

1. 73%
2. 25%
3. 47%
4. 3%
5. 99%
6. 0.12
7. 0.74
8. 0.27
9. 0.5
10. 0.06

Exercise 10.5

1. 25%
2. 20%
3. 45%
4. 16%
5. 30%
6. 96%
7. 40%
8. 41.7% (or $41.\dot{6}$% or $41\frac{2}{3}$%)
9. 75%
10. 5%

Exercise 11.1

1. 8
2. 10
3. 450
4. 7.2
5. 45g
6. £90
7. £8
8. 150 km
9. 27
10. 90

Exercise 11.2

1. 225
2. 598
3. 44p
4. 418
5. 138cm
6. 24 kg
7. £21
8. £56
9. 156 kg
10. £29

Exercise 11.3

1. 600 cm
2. 300 g
3. £40
4. 50 l
5. 1600 cm or 16 m
6. 500 km
7. £15
8. £300
9. £30
10. £64000

Exercise 11.4

1. 20%
2. 25%
3. 5%
4. 20%
5. 25%
6. 25%
7. 25%
8. 85%
9. 40%
10. 110%

Exercise 12.1

1. 8.82
2. 7.8
3. 2.25
4. 0.16
5. 3
6. 3.28
7. 112.5
8. 0.0 15
9. 1.924
10. 0.348

Exercise 12.2

1. 8
2. 400
3. 4.75
4. 12.025
5. 8.55
6. 6.1
7. 62.75
8. 26.8
9. 560
10. 144.3

Exercise 12.3

1. $\frac{7}{10}$
2. $\frac{3}{4}$
3. $\frac{12}{25}$
4. $\frac{1}{8}$
5. $\frac{17}{20}$
6. $\frac{16}{25}$
7. $1\frac{7}{20}$
8. $3\frac{1}{4}$
9. $1\frac{9}{20}$
10. $\frac{17}{40}$

Exercise 12.4

1. 0.3
2. 0.75
3. 0.4
4. 0.625
5. 0.6
6. 0.13
7. 0.425
8. 0.95
9. 0.32
10. 0.1875

Exercise 12.5

	Fraction	Decimal	Percentage
1.	$\frac{21}{50}$	0.42	42%
2.	$\frac{73}{200}$	0.365	36.5%
3.	$\frac{7}{20}$	0.35	35%
4.	$\frac{6}{25}$	0.24	24%
5.	$\frac{17}{25}$	0.68	68%
6.	$\frac{63}{100}$	0.63	63%
7.	$\frac{13}{20}$	0.65	65%
8.	$\frac{3}{20}$	0.15	15%
9.	$\frac{63}{200}$	0.315	31.5%
10.	$\frac{3}{16}$	0.1875	18.75%

Puzzle page 2

1. $\frac{2}{3}$
2. $2\frac{5}{8}$
3. $\frac{7}{8}$
4. $1\frac{7}{8}$
5. $2\frac{7}{8}$
6. 7.5
7. 0.75
8. 57%
9. 20%
10. $1\frac{3}{8}$
11. 24
12. 27
13. 45%
14. 35%

He was partial to fractions.

Exercise 13.1

1. 5
2. 10
3. 25
4. 30
5. 5
6. 3
7. 11.1
8. 4
9. $\frac{1}{2}$
10. 3000

Exercise 13.2

1. £33
2. £6
3. £72
4. 8
5. £4
6. 14°C
7. 282
8. 98%
9. 95%
10. 19

Exercise 13.3

1. mean: 6
   mode: 4
   median: 5
2. mean: 14
   mode: 12
   median: 12
3. mean: 11
   mode: 9
   median: 10.5 or $10\frac{1}{2}$
4. mean: 40
   mode: 38
   median: 40
5. mean: 11
   mode: 10, 13
   median: 11.5 or $11\frac{1}{2}$
6. mean: 9
   mode: 9
   median: 9
7. mean: $3\frac{1}{2}$
   mode: none
   median: 3
8. mean: 6cm
   mode: 6cm
   median:6cm
9. mean: 1.6m
   mode: 1.8m
   median: 1.7m
10. mean: 6.35kg
    mode: none
    median: 6kg

Exercise 13.4

1. 10
2. 7
3. 23
4. 4
5. 19
6. 0.19
7. $8\frac{1}{2}$
8. 6.5km
9. 0.9cm
10. 13.7kg

Exercise 14.1

1. 346p
2. 510p
3. 42p
4. 1788p
5. 500p
6. £6.00 or £6
7. £7.52
8. £3.80
9. £20.34
10. £0.32

Exercise 14.2

1. £11.47
2. £81 or £81.00
3. £125
4. £11.27
5. £3.40
6. £14.70
7. £4.50
8. 8 months
9. £13.25
10. £86.15

Exercise 14.3

1. 86p/500g
   71p/500g
   best value: 1kg
2. 87p/100g
   90p/100g
   best value: 100g
3. 10p/sticker
   6p/sticker
   best value: 150 stickers
4. 30p/bar
   27p/bar
   best value: pack of 8
5. 13p/100g
   12p/100g
   best value: 10kg
6. 8p/100g
   8p/100g
   best value: both the same
7. 21p/100g
   22p/100g
   20p/100g
   18p/100g
8. 1.5kg, 700g, 300g, 500g
9. £18.53
   (6x1.5kg + 1x700g + 1x300g)
10. 10.8kg

Exercise 14.4

1. €455
2. £200
3. 96 Francs
4. £1=$2.40
5. £14.58
6. $126
7. £75
8. 2.2p
9. $22500
10. £1.33

Exercise 15.1

1. 14
2. 180
3. 8
4. 168
5. 300
6. 20
7. 520 or 522
8. 2880
9. 8.5 or $8\frac{1}{2}$
10. 13

Exercise 15.2

1. Half past seven am
   7:30am
2. Six o'clock pm
   6:00pm
3. Five minutes to one pm
   12:55pm
4. Quarter to three pm
   2:45pm
5. Fourteen minutes to five pm
   4:46pm
6. Three minutes to two pm
   1:57pm
7. Quarter past five am
   5:15am
8. Eighteen minutes past eleven am
   11:18am
9. Twenty (minutes) past nine am
   9:20am
10. Twenty (minutes) to four pm
    3:40pm

Exercise 15.3

1. 07:22
2. 11:56
3. 17:24
4. 00:03
5. 21:45
6. 12:06pm
7. 6:30pm
8. 6:50am
9. 12:20am
10. 9:15pm

Exercise 15.4

1. $\frac{3}{4}$
2. $\frac{1}{6}$
3. $\frac{1}{4}$
4. $\frac{1}{3}$
5. $\frac{5}{8}$
6. $\frac{1}{12}$
7. 50%
8. 25%
9. 25%
10. 33%

Exercise 16.1

1. 12 h 45 min
2. 6h 20 min
3. 11 hours
4. 11 days
5. 14 days 3 h
6. 10 years 3 months
7. 16 years 5 months
8. 6 weeks 2 days 19h
9. 4 weeks 2 hours
10. 9 h 6 min 20 s

Exercise 16.2

1. 1 h 25 min
2. 1 h 45 min
3. 1 h 34 min
4. 2 days 18 h
5. 1 day 21 h
6. 1 weeks 6 days
7. 4 weeks 4 days
8. 2 weeks 6 days 15 h
9. 35 min 50s
10. 1 h 28 min 37 s

Exercise 16.3

1. 24 hours / 1 day
2. 6 h 15 min
3. 17 h 20 min
4. 48 h 45 min / 2 days 45 min
5. 4 years
6. 11 years 8 months
7. 28 years 6 months
8. 12 days 16 hours
9. 13 days 6 hours
10. 22 days 8 h 40 min

Exercise 16.4

1. 2 h 10 min
2. 1 h 20 min
3. 1 h 20 min
4. 1 h 24 min
5. 1 day 13 h
6. 1 day 10 h
7. 2 days 11 h
8. 10 months
9. 2 years 5 months
10. 1 h 16 min 19 s

Exercise 16.5

1. 1946
2. 2032
3. 9 years 4 months
4. 9 years 6 months
5. 2 years 10 months
6. 44 hours
7. 2 hours 25 min
8. 8 hours 45 min
9. 30%
10. 4 min 30 s

Exercise 17.1

1. 13BC
2. 1BC
3. 320BC
4. 12AD
5. 17th Century AD
6. 17th
7. 21st
8. 21st
9. 19th
10. 7^{th}BC

Exercise 17.2

1. 7:47am
2. 0949
3. 15:04
4. 7:41am
5. 3:37pm
6. 8:35am
7. 8:44am
8. 13:20
9. 14:10
10. 4:12pm

Exercise 17.3

1. 08:11
2. 9 min
3. 40 min
4. 07:51
5. 07:27
6. 08:21
7. 08:36
8. 07:41
9. 09:00
10. 08:14

Exercise 17.4

1. 4:00am
2. 0200
3. 7:40pm
4. 6am
5. 11:00am
6. 2:00pm
7. 5:00am
8. 10:30am
9. 11pm
10. 7:00pm

Puzzle Page 3

1. 18
2. 17
3. 16
4. 525
5. 365
6. 72
7. 20
8. 11:20pm
9. 8:48pm
10. 8:58am
11. 8:48am
12. 15

All the others are weak days.

Exercise 18.1

1. 1000
2. 1000
3. 100
4. 10
5. 1000
6. 10 000
7. 1000
8. 1000
9. 0.1
10. 1000 000

Exercise 18.2

1. 0.023
2. 4.03
3. 547
4. 75
5. 9.52
6. 2100
7. 630
8. 8400
9. 0.0502
10. 3000 000

Exercise 18.3

1. 12
2. 3
3. 2.5
4. 27
5. 15
6. 96
7. 2
8. 32
9. 1.25
10. 70

Exercise 18.4

1. 30
2. 1.8
3. 3
4. 36
5. 11
6. 20
7. 15
8. 4
9. 125
10. 3.3 or $3\frac{1}{3}$

Exercise 19.1

1. 4cm, 40mm
2. 2.3cm, 23mm
3. 0.6cm, 6mm
4. 2.05cm, 20.5mm
5. 2.5cm, 25mm
6. 55mph
7. 20ml
8. 33ml
9. 500g, 0.5kg
10. 1050g, 1.05kg

Exercise 19.2

1. 30°C
2. -11°C (accept -10°C or -12°C)
3. 16°C
4. 3°C (accept 2°C or 4°C)
5. 37°C (accept 36°C)
6. 5
7. 4
8. 2
9. 28°
10. 13°(accept 12°C or 14°C)

Exercise 19.3

1. 28.1kg
2. 2.3 ℓ
3. 0.7m or 70cm
4. 13
5. 16.3kg
6. 1.48m
7. 100
8. 6.3kg
9. 120km
10. 20

Exercise 19.4

1. (1,4)
2. (4,6)
3. (6,3)
4. (5,1)
5. (-2,6)
6. (0,4)
7. (5,2)
8. (-6,0)
9. (-4,-4)
10. (2,-4)

Exercise 20.1

1. B, C
2. A, D
3. 180°
4. 90°
5. 360°
6. CD
7. AB
8. D
9. B
10. E

Exercise 20.2

1. 60°
2. 45°
3. 135°
4. 80°
5. 56°
6. 55°
7. 40°
8. 139°
9. 135°
10. 60°

Exercise 20.3

1. 60°
2. 120°
3. 135°
4. 135°
5. 45°
6. 64°
7. 116°
8. 108°
9. 108°
10. 72°

Exercise 20.4

1. 40°
2. 60°
3. 60°
4. 65°
5. 122°
6. 38°
7. 110°
8. 135°
9. 105°
10. 70°

Exercise 21.1

1. regular pentagon
2. irregular quadrilateral
3. regular heptagon
4. irregular hexagon
5. irregular heptagon
6. irregular decagon
7. irregular pentagon
8. regular decagon
9. regular nonagon
10. irregular octagon

Exercise 21.2

1. square
2. 60°
3. rhombus
4. 120°, 60°, 60°
5. arrowhead they are acute, kite they are obtuse.
6. parallelogram
7. parallelograms the equal angles are opposite, trapeziums the equal angles are adjacent (next to each other).
8. rhombus
9. triangle (right angle, scalene)
10. square, rectangle, rhombus, trapezium, kite, arrowhead

Exercise 21.3

1. circumference
2. semicircle
3. radius
4. diameter
5. circumference
6. radius = 11m
   diameter = 22m
7. radius = 6 cm
   diameter = 12cm
8. radius = 17cm
   diameter = 34cm
9. Ellipse not circle
10. Diameter goes through centre/ chord does not go through centre of circle.

Exercise 22.1

1. 18cm
2. 20cm
3. 12cm
4. 20cm
5. 16cm
6. 20cm
7. 48cm
8. 21.6km
9. 28m
10. 40cm

Exercise 22.2

1. $12cm^2$
2. $20m^2$
3. $9cm^2$
4. $25.92km^2$
5. $121m^2$
6. $1500m^2$
7. $250m^2$
8. $162m^2$
9. $5000ft^2$
10. $463.6m^2$

Exercise 22.3

1. $18cm^2$
2. $36cm^2$
3. $18cm^2$
4. $14cm^2$
5. $13.5cm^2$
6. $45cm^2$
7. $10cm^2$
8. $12m^2$
9. $550m^2$
10. $0.42cm^2$

Exercise 22.4

1. $21m^2$
2. $330m^2$
3. $224cm^2$
4. $69m^2$
5. $96m^2$
6. $10m^2$
7. 64
8. $7000cm^2$
9. $48cm^2$
10. $90cm^2$

Exercise 23.1

1. 7cm
2. 15cm
3. 20cm
4. 15cm
5. 12cm
6. 7cm
7. 10cm
8. 12cm
9. 12cm
10. 8cm

Exercise 23.2

1. 48cm
2. 12cm
3. $25cm^2$
4. $75cm^2$
5. 26cm
6. $6cm^2$
7. 17cm
8. $4.03cm^2$
9. $4.41cm^2$
10. $7.5cm^2$

Exercise 23.3

1. 3
2. 4
3. 2
4. 1
5. 2
6. 1
7. 0
8. 5
9. 1
10. 0

Exercise 23.4

1. 3
2. 4
3. 2
4. 1
5. 2
6. 1
7. 1
8. 5
9. 1
10. 2

Exercise 24.1

1. Square based pyramid
   5, 8, 5
2. Cuboid
   6, 12, 8
3. Pentagonal pyramid
   6, 10, 6
4. Cube
   6, 12, 8
5. Sphere
   1, 0, 0
6. Triangular prism
   5, 9, 6
7. Triangular pyramid
   4, 6, 4
8. Pentagonal prism
   7, 15, 10
9. Cone
   2, 1, 1
10. Cylinder
    3, 2, 0

Exercise 24.2

1. 24 cm^3
2. 36 cm^3
3. 192 cm^3
4. 224 cm^3
5. 175 cm^3
6. 960 cm^3
7. 144 cm^3
8. 283 cm^3
9. 125 cm^3
10. 228 cm^3

Exercise 24.3

1. 150 cm^2
2. 24 cm^2
3. 13.5 cm^2
4. 132 cm^2
5. 56 cm^2
6. 72 cm^2
7. 72 cm^2
8. 52 cm^2
9. 672 cm^2
10. 240 cm^2

Exercise 24.4

1. Trapezium prism (accept trapezoid)
2. Cube
3. Octahedron
4. Hexagonal prism
5. Cone
6. Triangular prism
7. Triangular pyramid or tetrahedron
8. Cuboid
9. Square based pyramid
10. Pentagonal pyramid

Puzzle Page 4

1. 54
2. 144
3. 127
4. 118
5. 62
6. 132
7. 172
8. 4
9. 23
10. 25
11. 112
12. 116

Stand in the corner it's 90 degrees there.

Exercise 25.1

1. East
2. North
3. North-west
4. North
5. North-west
6. North-east
7. North-east
8. East
9. North
10. South-west

Exercise 25.2

1. BF
2. R
3. Q
4. BC
5. AZ
6. BF
7. L
8. BP
9. AG
10. BA

Exercise 25.3

1. 6 km/h
2. 37.5 km/h
3. 15 mph
4. 190 km/h
5. 260.4 m
6. $16.\dot{6}$ or 16.7 m/s or 60km/h
7. 4 km/h
8. 5 km
9. 40 min
10. 15 600 000 km/h

Exercise 25.4

1. 70s or 1 min 10 s
2. 80m
3. They stop
4. 140m
5. 2m/s
6. 2m/s
7. 0m/s
8. End of trip is faster
9. Line is steeper
10. 4m/s

Exercise 26.1

1. 2:3
2. 8:5:3
3. 2:1
4. 7:16
5. $\frac{1}{3}$
6. $\frac{3}{13}$
7. $\frac{3}{8}$
8. $\frac{5}{12}$
9. 75%
10. 40%

Exercise 26.2

1. 660
2. 90g
3. 8
4. £63
5. 35cm, 10cm
6. 12
7. 20kg
8. 273
9. 750ml
10. 1:3

Exercise 26.3

1. 280 km
2. 15cm
3. 10ft:3cm
4. 40ft
5. 8cm
6. 72cm
7. 6ft
8. 8km
9. 160ft
10. 1:20

Exercise 26.4

1. 12
2. 40
3. 40
4. 200km
5. £1500
6. 95
7. 10min
8. 20min
9. 1 mile
10. 3

Exercise 27.1

1. certain
2. even chance
3. likely
4. unlikely
5. 0
6. 1
7. 0.5 or $\frac{1}{2}$
8. A
9. Fair
10. unfair

Exercise 27.2

1. $\frac{1}{2}$
2. $\frac{1}{5}$
3. $\frac{1}{4}$
4. $\frac{3}{13}$
5. $\frac{1}{26}$
6. $\frac{1}{8}$
7. $\frac{3}{8}$
8. $\frac{1}{3}$
9. $\frac{1}{6}$
10. $\frac{2}{3}$

Exercise 27.3

1. HH. HT, TT
2. AB, AC, AD, BC, BD, CD
3. BB, BR, BG, RB, RR, RG, GB, GR, GG
4. BB, BR, BG, RB, RG, GB, GR
5. BB, BR, BG, RG
6. 6 (SP, SJ, ST, PJ, PT, JT)
7. 12
8. 560
9. 15
10. 20

Exercise 27.4

1. $\frac{1}{4}$
2. $\frac{1}{36}$
3. $\frac{35}{36}$
4. $\frac{5}{36}$
5. $\frac{1}{2}$
6. $\frac{1}{10}$
7. $\frac{2}{11}$
8. $\frac{1}{15}$
9. $\frac{5}{14}$
10. $\frac{13}{28}$

Exercise 28.1

1. A
2. 6
3. 2
4. 2
5. Guinea pig
6. 23
7. $\frac{4}{9}$
8. 33
9. 2
10. $\frac{1}{5}$

Exercise 28.2

1. 26 miles
2. 106 miles
3. 17 miles
4. 140 miles
5. 40 miles
6. Walsall and Wolverhampton
7. 56 miles
8. 53 miles
9. 400 miles
10. 145 miles

Exercise 28.3

1. 24
2. Kiwi fruit
3. Apple and orange
4. 8
5. 13
6. $\frac{1}{6}$
7. $\frac{3}{10}$
8. 42
9. 20%
10. 47%

Exercise 28.4

1. $\frac{1}{8}$
2. 240
3. 120
4. 960
5. 37.5%
6. 6 hours
7. 2 hours
8. 9 hours
9. 1 hour
10. 3 hours

Exercise 29.1

1. 52cm
2. 280 days
3. 86cm (accept 87)
4. 78cm (accept 77 – 81cm)
5. 9cm
6. 4.5kg
7. 9kg
8. 180kg
9. 11lb
10. 22lb

Exercise 29.2

1. Tomaz
2. Martha
3. 35
4. Nikhil
5. Amy and Ayo
6. 300
7. 175
8. Monday
9. 225
10. 1050

Exercise 29.3

1.

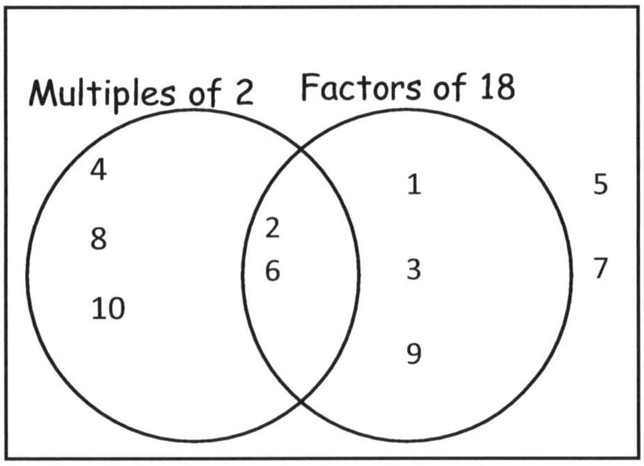

2. Owl, sparrow or robin (accept Dodo or Great Auk)
3. Extinct, had constant body temperature, no wings
4. Pinta giant tortoise or silver trout
5. Giant auk
6. 52
7. 60
8. 22
9. 43%
10. 44

Exercise 29.4

1. £1.70
2. £1.60
3. 50p
4. 20p
5. £2.10
6. Is it red?
7. Staples
8. Does it have long sleeves?
9. Arachnid
10. Crustacean

Exercise 30.1

1. 19
2. 4
3. 13
4. 7
5. 30
6. 8
7. 11
8. 63
9. 4
10. 3

Exercise 30.2

1. A= l x w or A = lw
2. c = b + g or c = g + b
3. c = 3.50 + 2m
4. c = 1.3v
5. c = 40 + 30m
6. 2a + 2b
7. 2a - b
8. 4a
9. 4a + 2b
10. a

Exercise 30.2

1. 14
2. 13
3. 15
4. 2
5. 81
6. a
7. c
8. b
9. p
10. r

Exercise 30.4

1. 26
2. 36
3. 84
4. £8.50
5. £170
6. 220 min or 3h 40 min
7. £15
8. £2250
9. 57 km/h
10. 21500 J

Exercise 30.5a

1. variable
2. coefficient
3. coefficient
4. variable
5. constant
6. L
7. U
8. L
9. U
10. U

Exercise 30.5b

1. 8a
2. 7w
3. 5a-b
4. $8d^2+5d$
5. $15x^3+2x^2+4x+11$
6. $6z^2+z+4$
7. $45b^2-4b+2t+s$
8. 21w+15wx-3x
9. 70q+5qr
10. $5s^3$

Exercise 31.1

1. st
2. 2ab
3. $4w^2$
4. $14y^2$
5. $27yz^2$
6. $18s^2t$
7. $5y^2z$
8. 22a
9. $4r^2s$
10. $27t^2v$

Exercise 31.2a

1. n^2
2. $4s^2$
3. 3rs
4. 7p
5. 11a
6. 5
7. 6xy
8. $7b^4$
9. $\frac{3s}{u}$
10. $3x^5y^2$

Exercise 31.2b

1. 20s
2. $15a^2$
3. $16e^2$
4. $7w^2$
5. $18d^2$
6. $6a^2+2ab$
7. 16ab
8. $10s^2t + 7t$
9. $42q^2 - 2q$
10. $72y^2$

Exercise 31.3

1. 11
2. 3
3. 7
4. 4
5. 15
6. 32
7. 14
8. $1\frac{1}{2}$ or 1.5
9. 4
10. 4

Exercise 31.4

1.	2x + 1	21
2.	6x-1	71
3.	2x + 23	53
4.	3x - 7	293
5.	5x - 25	75
6.	3x + 56 = 62	2
7.	5x - 22 = 78	20
8.	$\frac{x}{4}$ + 17 = 47	120
9.	R + 2 = 12÷2	4
10.	2x + 22 = 60 or x + x + 22 = 60	£19

Puzzle Page 5

1. 56
2. 126
3. 72
4. 12
5. 6
6. 240
7. 96
8. 230
9. 60
10. 9
11. 36
12. 3

x was always worth ten.

Verbal Reasoning Answers

Exercise 1.1

1. shoe
2. slope
3. honesty
4. shape
5. London
6. Wednesday
7. Nile
8. Headteacher
9. Father
10. Abstract

Exercise 1.2

1. He
2. them
3. our
4. it
5. her
6. his
7. himself
8. I
9. it
10. me

Exercise 1.3

1. the
2. a
3. the
4. the
5. a
6. no article is needed.
7. the
8. the
9. the
10. an

Exercise 2.1

1. listens
2. hits
3. like, hates
4. says
5. goes
6. carries
7. examines
8. have become
9. is, was
10. seems, will

Exercise 2.2

1. am
2. is
3. are
4. has
5. are
6. are
7. Is
8. has
9. are
10. is

Exercise 2.3

1. found
2. flew
3. spoke
4. lit
5. blew
6. slid
7. went
8. was
9. played
10. caught

Exercise 2.4

1. will
2. –
3. going
4. will go
5. working
6. is
7. –
8. be
9. going (accept off)
10. will (accept do)

Exercise 3.1

1. reliable
2. respectable or respectful
3. shining
4. thoughtful
5. thankful
6. resentful
7. enjoyable
8. selfish
9. useful or useable
10. pouring

Exercise 3.2

1. colder
2. worst
3. hardest
4. scarier
5. faster
6. better
7. tallest
8. bigger, bigger, biggest
9. curlier
10. least

Exercise 3.3

1. quickly
2. just
3. usually
4. carefully
5. consequently
6. lazily
7. happily
8. easily
9. soon
10. almost

Exercise 3.4

1. will
2. –
3. going
4. – or going
5. working
6. was
7. –
8. be
9. going
10. will

Exercise 4.1

1. until
2. however
3. because
4. when
5. so
6. although
7. because
8. then
9. after
10. because

Exercise 4.2

1. over, in, under
2. before, of, as, against
3. after, next to, by, about, during
4. into, within, tomorrow, outside
5. down
6. against
7. of
8. on
9. in
10. on

Exercise 5.1

1. **A**re you free next **W**ednesday?
2. **T**he temperature was minus two degrees **Celcius**.
3. "**P**lease come to my party," said **R**obert.
4. **H**e asked the teacher how to calculate a mean, "**L**ike this," the teacher replied.
5. **S**he bought 3 kilograms of meat from the **F**ine **C**uts **B**utchers.
6. **T**he hospital warned that car parking was limited on **S**outh **S**treet.
7. **A**n adverb is a word that describes a verb.
8. **T**he **D**uke and **D**uchess of **C**ambridge's first child is **P**rince **W**illiam.
9. **F**inally, **M**r **S**mith said that his daughter could go to the party in **L**ondon.
10. **H**e was able to speak **F**rench and **S**wahili fluently, which was very helpful when visiting **E**ast **A**frica.

Exercise 5.2

1. .
2. ?
3. ?
4. !
5. ...
6. !
7. .
8. .
9. .
10. !

6.1 Clauses and Phrases

1. P
2. C
3. C
4. P
5. C
6. P
7. C
8. P
9. P
10. P

6.2 Types of clause

1. S
2. S
3. S
4. M
5. S
6. noun
7. adverbial
8. relative
9. relative
10. relative

6.3 Types of phrase

1. N
2. P – Adv
3. P – Adj
4. N
5. P – Adj
6. P – Adv
7. N
8. N
9. P – Adv
10. Adj

6.4 Fronted Adverbials

1. Nervously, he peered around the corner
2. To visit my friend, I went into town.
3. Out of nowhere, the monster appeared.
4. Without warning, the fire alarm went off.
5. Behind the shed, there is a family of hedgehogs.
6. t
7. m
8. m
9. t
10. p

Exercise 7.1

1. P
2. C
3. C
4. P
5. MC
6. P
7. SO
8. P
9. MC
10. SO

Exercise 7.2

1. Ruth loved all food, particularly pasta.
2. C.S. Lewis, who is mostly known for the Narnia Chronicles, wrote many books.
3. Anthony wanted to play with his friends, though he really needed to finish his homework.
4. The biology course, which is very intensive, is finishing on Friday.
5. Since they installed the new run, the hens have been laying lots of eggs.
6. You must wash your hands, even if they look clean, after taking the rubbish out.
7. He loved reading all books, though historical adventure books were his favourite.
8. Although many considered themselves knowledgeable, the results revealed a lack of knowledge.
9. By the time we got home, the movie we really wanted to watch had finished.
10. In a food chain, not all the energy taken in by an organism passes to the next organism.

Exercise 7.3

1. Please buy some cheese, ham, apples, bananas and bread on your way home.
2. Please can I have the large, red book?
3. The colours of the spectrum are: red, orange, yellow, green, blue, indigo and violet.
4. For homework you must complete: the definitions, crossword and practice questions.
5. Anyone who wishes to succeed as a scientist must have: dedication, excellent time management skills, good knowledge and an ability to think logically.
6. Finally Mark, Matthew, Jason, Ansha and Diya arrived.
7. I tried her home, mobile and work numbers, but could not contact her.
8. Choices of meal included: spaghetti, fried rice, stir fry, and sausages and eggs.
9. Go past the old church, turn left at the end of the road, turn right at the park and my house is third on the left.
10. She did lots of afterschool activities including: netball, science club, computing and film club.

Exercise 7.4

1. "Please can I go to the party," he begged.
2. She lives in Burnham, Buckinghamshire.
3. "Hi, how are you?"
4. However, I am in good health.
5. Wait, I will think about it.
6. Yes, I would like a cup of tea please.
7. "They have forecast rain," he reported.
8. The cyclone hit Darwin, Australia.
9. We moved in December, 2011.
10. Unfortunately, we do not have enough time.

Exercise 8.1

1. The potion contained: frogs legs, snails and unicorn horns.
2. There was only one way he could pass: he had to practice every day.
3. I have invited the following people to my party: Amy, Simona and Andrea.
4. You only have one choice: leave while you can.
5. You must bring to the exam: two pencils, a rubber, a pencil, sharpener, a bottle of water and a small snack.
6. You must persevere and try hard. Remember the quotation: "Aim for the moon. If you miss, you may hit a star."
7. Hurry: I can't wait long.
8. Remember what our teacher always said: "Always treat others with respect."
9. There are many gaming platforms such as: the Wii, Nintendo DS, X-box, the PlayStation and the PC.
10. Punctuation: it makes language easier to understand.

Exercise 8.2

1. No
2. Yes
3. No
4. Yes
5. Yes
6. No (should be colon)
7. No
8. Yes
9. Yes
10. No

Exercise 8.3

1. For lunch you can choose ham, cheese or chicken sandwiches, tea, coffee or hot chocolate, and apple pie, chocolate brownie or ice-cream sundae.
2. For her school project, she had to write a biography. She could choose from: Wolfgang Amadeus Mozart, the composer, Florence Nightingale, the nurse, Christopher Columbus, the explorer or Edward Jenner, the doctor.
3. In the meeting today we have Richard Smith, Curtin University, Andrew McGowan, Yale, Alister McGrath, Oxford University and Patrick Flynn, Cambridge University.
4. Cows are very useful as they give us milk, which contains lots of nutrients, meat is high in protein and leather which makes the best shoes.
5. For Christmas I sent cards to many places, such as: Dodoma, Tanzania, Tansen, Nepal and Perth, Australia.
6. She had lots of homework including: an essay for English, a lab report for Science, a past paper for Maths and another essay for History.
7. Here are the directions: leave the M4 at Junction 7, turn left at the round-about and then left at Langley High Street.
8. When trying to work out who to dress up as for book-week, he considered: Harry Potter; Charlie Bucket, Charlie and the Chocolate Factory; Peter, The Narnia Chronicles or Aslan also from the Narnia Chronicles.
9. Some places I still want to visit in Europe are: Prague, Czech Republic; Berlin, Germany; Copenhagen, Denmark; Vienna, Austria and the Greek Islands.
10. For parents evening, my parents needed to see: Dr Simpson, Science; Mr Maughan, English; Miss Cleghorne, History; Mr Groves, Maths; Mme Moreau, French and Mr Money, Business Studies.

Exercise 9.1

1. Dad's pen.
2. The dog's lead.
3. The shirt's collar.
4. The bridesmaids' dresses.
5. The family's car.
6. His boss' wife.
7. James' computer.
8. The children's party.
9. The box's edge.
10. The songs' lyrics.

Exercise 9.2

1. isn't
2. we're
3. who'll
4. I've
5. I'm
6. could've
7. they're
8. where'd
9. let's
10. they'd

Exercise 9.3

1. It's
2. its
3. it's
4. its
5. It's
6. Its
7. its
8. its
9. it's
10. it's

Exercise 10.1

1. "Are we there yet," they chorused.
2. "What do you want to drink," he was asked.
3. He really enjoyed reading "The Magician's Nephew," by C.S. Lewis.
4. "I don't believe you," she said, "you never tell the truth."
5. As Nelson Mandela once said, "Education is the most powerful weapon, which you can use to change the world."
6. "Excuse me," I said, "do you have the time?"
7. Anna suggested that "Frozen" would be a fun movie to watch.
8. She read so many of the "Secret Seven" by Enid Blyton, she considered the characters her friends.
9. "Mum said, you can go now," Aunty Pat said.
10. "My favourite book is Harry Potter and the Philosopher's Stone, what's yours?" he asked.

Exercise 10.2

1. She needed a chest x-ray.
2. They had been married for fifty-four years when she died.
3. There was a break-in at the local shopping centre.
4. Post-1900 there has been a national education system in England.
5. For sale: a little, used boat. (The boat is little but used a lot). no hyphen
6. He appeared stern but was actually a warm-hearted man.
7. He's a two year-old child. Can also have a hyphen between two and year
8. Please fasten your seat-belt.
9. They had a second-hand cabinet in the lounge room. (optional lounge-room)
10. She needed to buy a present for her mother-in-law's birthday.

Exercise 10.3

1. B
2. B
3. C
4. A
5. C
6. A
7. C
8. A
9. C
10. D

Exercise 11.1

1. fear
2. limb
3. own
4. ten
5. sigh
6. trough
7. though, although
8. wool
9. piece
10. snow

Exercise 11.2

1. Claire, custard, creams, crispy, cookies, cupboard
2. Mike, meandered, magical, moist
3. We, went, Windsor, whispered
4. Cooked, crunchy, cream candies (not Charlie and chocolate)
5. circus, skills, sent, spine (not shivers)
6. stones
7. flew
8. reared
9. prepared
10. drive

Exercise 11.3

1. grew, grew, flew, flew
2. deal, read, sheet, leave
3. cow, found, ground (not meadow)
4. try, light, fire, nightfall
5. felt, depressed, restless
6. here, there, everywhere
7. inkling, it, is. Imp
8. beast, sea, seek, feast
9. sow, mow, meadow
10. frail, trailed, glade

Exercise 11.4

1. deal, file, dial
2. light, helped, plant, upright
3. black, sack, back
4. dawn, sun, down
5. strong, swing
6. pitter, patter
7. clopped, hard, wood
8. hiker, near, moor
9. mash, dish
10. storm, worm

Exercise 11.5

1. whizzed
2. bump
3. cough
4. croaking
5. crackling
6. creak
7. murmured
8. rustling
9. zipped
10. pop

Exercise 12.1

1. climb
2. solemn
3. receipt
4. reign
5. wrap
6. listen
7. choir
8. assign
9. knitted
10. built

Exercise 12.2

1. madam
2. level
3. peep
4. kayak
5. minim
6. tide
7. knits
8. desserts
9. smart
10. stang

Exercise 12.3

1. interesting
2. wonderful
3. envelope
4. dictionary
5. comfortable
6. golden, valuable
7. exceptional
8. confident
9. calendar
10. solution, problem

Exercise 12.4

1. recital
2. aces
3. kitchen
4. stove
5. antler
6. organist
7. stew
8. thaw
9. siren
10. elbow

Exercise 13.1

1. idle
2. tranquil
3. novice
4. prohibit
5. remorse
6. just
7. concur
8. prosperous
9. hardworking
10. spontaneous

Exercise 13.2

1. feeble
2. vacant
3. usual
4. volume
5. besides
6. hilarious
7. sombre
8. blossom
9. permit
10. protect

Exercise 13.3

1. confused
2. placate
3. essential
4. distant
5. require
6. mask
7. cargo
8. fable
9. esteem
10. sag

Exercise 13.4

1. abundant
2. competent
3. abandon
4. abrupt
5. nuisance
6. wrath
7. vain
8. option
9. demolish
10. robust

Exercise 14.1

1. opponent
2. estimate
3. opaque
4. lenient
5. malice
6. phony
7. peripheral
8. eager
9. anxious
10. stabilise

Exercise 14.2

1. complex
2. juvenile
3. stale
4. follow
5. leisure
6. scarce
7. blame
8. cruel
9. poverty
10. clumsy

Exercise 14.3

1. dull
2. active
3. soothe
4. drenching
5. transform
6. dismiss
7. vacate
8. understandable
9. erroneous
10. enhance

Exercise 14.4

1. careful
2. ashamed
3. chaotic
4. humble
5. insult
6. unite
7. unique
8. villain
9. comic
10. cloudy

Exercise 15.1

1. hall
2. wrench
3. tomato
4. rose
5. lime
6. crocodile
7. brogue
8. bat
9. larch
10. envelope

Exercise 15.2

1. radiographer
2. articles
3. sentence
4. barge
5. biology
6. fork
7. scientist
8. cell
9. quarry
10. brick

Exercise 15.3

1. box
2. floor
3. badminton
4. soup
5. loss
6. bacteria
7. reptile
8. rig
9. toast
10. day

Exercise 16.1

11. Tokyo
12. potato
13. neck
14. paper
15. water
16. moon
17. November
18. wind
19. Africa
20. pacify

Exercise 16.2

11. pills
12. modern
13. know
14. stab
15. tailed
16. eight
17. slept
18. sword
19. coal
20. weakly

Exercise 17.1

1. fair, fair
2. saw, sore, sore
3. lessen, lesson
4. flaw, floor
5. allowed, aloud
6. principal, principles
7. fowl, foul
8. mourning, morning
9. flour, mousse
10. compliment, licence

Exercise 17.2

1. aisle
2. coarse
3. idle
4. pour
5. heir
6. sighed
7. mayor
8. lead
9. barren
10. urn

Exercise 18.1

1. content
2. permit
3. letter
4. fine
5. tune
6. study
7. lead
8. ball
9. tear
10. foot

Exercise 18.2

1. stamp
2. sink
3. swear
4. tart
5. close
6. match
7. bear
8. monitor
9. bark
10. down

Exercise 19.1

1. elsewhere
2. because
3. today
4. button
5. saucepan
6. fortnight
7. forgive
8. keyhole
9. armchair
10. cutlet

Exercise 19.2

1. back
2. fire
3. any
4. out
5. tea
6. for
7. head
8. sand
9. door
10. wood

Exercise 19.3

1. handsome
2. rather
3. soon
4. heat
5. damage
6. island
7. massage
8. nowhere
9. errand
10. budget

Exercise 20.1

1. antonym
2. character
3. platform
4. pilot
5. eclipse
6. evaporate
7. fickle
8. query
9. sandwich
10. volatile

Exercise 20.2

1. well
2. rug
3. each or ache
4. lend
5. amen
6. are
7. all
8. act
9. gum
10. met

Exercise 21.1

1. words, worth
2. holidays, sleeping
3. your, all
4. England, London
5. cinema, the
6. that, for
7. and, a
8. girl, the
9. huge, lemonade
10. his, he

Exercise 21.2

1. The train should be here soon. / The train should soon be here.
2. They are studying because they have a test tomorrow.
3. Her birthday party is tomorrow evening. / Tomorrow evening is her birthday party.
4. My parents sent me a postcard.
5. Children grow taller as they get older. / Children get taller as they grow older.
6. The children loved the day at the zoo.

7. I wonder who started that rumour. / Who started that rumour, I wonder.
8. He hurt his hand when he fell. / He fell when he hurt his hand.
9. We had very little snow this winter. / This winter we had very little snow.
10. She speaks three languages fluently. / She fluently speaks three languages.

Exercise 22.1

1. as
2. see
3. some
4. wings
5. alarm
6. bathroom
7. flowers
8. snow
9. card
10. fish

Exercise 22.2

1. all
2. seaside
3. found
4. car
5. the
6. morning
7. had
8. of
9. exams
10. population

Exercise 23.1

1. classified
2. features
3. hair
4. control
5. is
6. enabled
7. live
8. characteristics
9. having
10. breathe

Exercise 23.2

1. there
2. tyre
3. hole
4. night
5. see
6. wondered
7. heard
8. great
9. straight
10. rain

Exercise 24.1

1. have
2. well
3. opened
4. slowly
5. out
6. been
7. extremely
8. accident
9. escaping
10. another

Exercise 24.2

1. are
2. situated
3. height
4. above
5. originate
6. variety
7. endangered
8. estimated
9. unique
10. nearly

Exercise 24.3

1. D
2. F
3. B
4. E
5. H
6. J
7. D
8. E
9. H
10. B

Exercise 25.1

1. season
2. drop
3. enough
4. cover
5. slip
6. control
7. accidents
8. blazing
9. scarves
10. chocolate

Exercise 25.2

1. received
2. checked
3. neighbours
4. their
5. suitable
6. valuable
7. opinion
8. comfortable
9. elegant
10. occasion

Exercise 26.1

1. Poetry, fiction
2. Prose, non-fiction
3. Prose, fiction
4. Poetry, fiction
5. Speech, to inform
6. Play-script, to entertain
7. Journal, to preserve / remember
8. Informative, to inform
9. Narrative, to entertain
10. Advertising, to persuade

Exercise 27.1

1. Introduction, books or joy
2. Beginnings
3. History or early writing
4. Material or medium
5. Papyrus or scroll
6. Parchment or vellum
7. Codex or codices
8. (Printing) press
9. Electronic books or e-book
10. Conclusion or future

Exercise 27.2

1. Strongly dislikes
2. Regugnant very strong term
3. A film covering something
4. To mark stark contrast with rich child
5. Thoughtless or cheap
6. Dislikes
7. To point out the condition of the car and their frustration.
8. To inform about the effect of diet
9. To emphasise the harm that an unhealthy diet can have
10. To emphasise the cold, miserable conditions

Exercise 27.3

1. c
2. b
3. a
4. a
5. d
6. c
7. a
8. d
9. c
10. b

Exercise 28.1

1. yellow, line 28
2. eyes moving, lines 8/9
3. insulted, line 10
4. Stuck out his tongue, line 23
5. Pulled Gepetto's wig off, line 27/28
6. Walk, line 23
7. Gepetto's nose, line 39
8. Angry, line 20
9. As his father, line 35
10. They were stiff, line 44

Exercise 28.2

1. c
2. b
3. a
4. c
5. c
6. b
7. c
8. c
9. c
10. a

Exercise 28.3

1. d
2. d
3. b
4. a
5. b
6. b
7. a
8. a
9. b
10. d
11. b
12. c
13. b
14. b
15. a
16. a
17. b
18. b
19. d
20. b

Exercise 29.1

1. (a) White lilies , pure as falling snow; (b)The air is like a mother's hand
3. Any two of: (a) Shake o'er my head thy slumb'rous wings: Nightfall is compared to something that flies. (b) Lulled by the breath of evening: The night air is compared to breath without using the word "like" or "as." (c) the low / Music of sleepy winds: winds is compared to music without using "like" or "as." (d) the prison-door unbars: implicitly compares waking consciousness to a closed prison-door.
5. Any three of: (a)silence of the summer night! (b) Alive with wistful murmurings (c) Enfold me in thy quiet might: (d) Tired roses, (e) Kind sleep (f) the weary world bereaves (g) Lulled by the breath of evening, (h) The peace of heaven is stealing now (i) the quiet stars / Look down with steadfast eloquence, (j) held the mute world's inmost sense
8. Peaceful
9. Simile (uses the work like)
10. Metaphor

Exercise 29.2

1. First three lines rhyme and last three lines rhyme.
2. clasps, crags, crooked or wrinkled, watches, walls
3. ‘close to the sun’ or ‘like a thunderbolt he falls’
4. first two lines and second two lines / aabb / rhyming couplets
5. any two of: (a) when, again, Croydon (b) flies, sings, (strings) (c) hitting, strings
6. hooty
7. growl
8. either cricket, came or pathetic pendulum
9. later, summer / yet, that, meant, cricket (the t’s give sense of a clock ticking)
10. when winter or going home

Exercise 30.1

1. the sun
2. lies the wintry sun a-bed and sleepyhead
3. the sun appears not to be active in winter
4. stars skies or cold candle
5. creates rhythm
   The cold candle also gives sense of cold c,c,c
6. No, it's not really cold, just portraying that even with the candle it is cold.
7. Covered with snow
8. Creates image of clouds sailing
9. The rainbow
10. The heavens (or the sky) are beautiful

Exercise 30.2

1. b
2. a
3. a
4. c
5. a
6. c
7. d
8. c
9. b
10. c

Verbal Reasoning (GL-style) Answers

1.1 Letter Sequences

1. R,U
2. N, R
3. A, Y
4. N, I
5. A, C
6. N, P
7. O, N
8. E, D
9. P, T
10. A, Z
11. G, G
12. BV, EX
13. EL, FN
14. MP, PS
15. HR, LP
16. EF, FG
17. IJ, KL
18. TS, RQ
19. UJ, ZQ
20. WS, RV

1.2 Analogies

1. PQ
2. TU
3. FD
4. HL
5. SR
6. DG
7. BX
8. YA
9. IJ
10. GF

1.3 Order of size

1. 3
2. thirteen
3. 3:00 p.m.
4. warm
5. year 1
6. small
7. bad
8. tens
9. London
10. mouse

1.4 Alphabet letters

1. F
2. Y
3. A
4. I
5. N
6. E
7. IT
8. IN
9. T
10. MN (either order)

1.5 Practice

1. KB, LZ
2. MQ, LS
3. NC, PB
4. KH, PF
5. GQ, MS
6. OP
7. KI
8. NR
9. XW
10. TW
11. sentence
12. six
13. third
14. March
15. day
16. H
17. V
18. O
19. O
20. S

2.1 Finish and Start
1. N
2. R
3. M
4. L
5. Y
6. G
7. F
8. T
9. D
10. F

2.2 Alphabetic Order
1. nectarine
2. dictionary
3. orange
4. juice
5. gift
6. plum
7. glass
8. pilot
9. line
10. oregano

2.3 Missing letters
1. SEE
2. TAG
3. SAW
4. TEN
5. RIB
6. HOP
7. AIR
8. HER
9. ACT
10. VAN

2.4 Hidden Words
1. need (cone, edge)
2. shin (hush, in)
3. till (until, later)
4. ship (checks, hippopotamuses)
5. them (truth, emerged)
6. lick (colic, kept)
7. dear (idea, required)
8. race (another ace)
9. wasp (was, polite)
10. chin (stitch, in)

2.5 Practice
1. T
2. K
3. R
4. Y
5. H
6. lawyer
7. muffins
8. maths
9. money
10. goat

11. PUT
12. HAM
13. AGE
14. LET
15. EAT
16. chin (reach, into)
17. kind (look, India)
18. sent (bass, entered)
19. went (show, entrant)
20. near (deadline, arrived)

3.1 Odd Two Out

1. rainbow, colour
2. clothes, hands
3. rice, pasta
4. ball, racquet
5. house, kitchen
6. reading, writing
7. hen, duck
8. hospital, patient
9. telephone, electricity
10. bread, toast

3.2 Synonyms

1. giggle
2. ill
3. pleased
4. freezing
5. magnify
6. intelligent, clever
7. chair, seat
8. glasses, tumblers
9. add, sum
10. make, create
11. bear
12. scamp
13. assume
14. frail
15. clear
16. kind, type
17. buoyant, cheerful
18. illicit, forbidden
19. glimpse, glance
20. fine, well

3.3 Antonyms

1. all
2. ambiguous
3. white
4. down
5. outside
6. present, past
7. right, left
8. talk, listen
9. few, many
10. food, drink
11. prolong
12. demolish
13. flourish
14. opening
15. fresh
16. cluster, isolate
17. wash, soil
18. attempt, ignore
19. jam, clear
20. maroon, rescue

3.4 Middle Words

1. SHOW
2. HARE
3. GLOW
4. CARE
5. COME
6. PAIR
7. COOK
8. MIND
9. TORE
10. LINE

3.5 Practice

1. tree, bush
2. school, classroom
3. sheep, horse
4. mouse, badger
5. gentleman, chap
6. scared, frightened
7. dear, expensive
8. rubbish, litter
9. thick, wide
10. thin, slim
11. rude, polite
12. sleep, awake
13. entree, dessert
14. stop, start
15. old, young
16. DEAR
17. RACK
18. READ
19. CLIP
20. BAND

4.1 Can(not) be made

1. fare
2. prod
3. lone
4. went
5. hail
6. dial
7. rain
8. gong
9. drum
10. sent

4.2 Compound Words

1. pass, port
2. sand, paper
3. eye, lid
4. hand, shake
5. finger, print
6. so, on
7. fat, her
8. sud, den
9. butter, fly
10. check, up

4.3 Rearranging Words

1. ducks
2. care
3. fear
4. clip
5. flag
6. plum
7. some
8. rise
9. tail
10. rose
11. dim
12. fun
13. sow
14. gel
15. noun
16. fuel
17. rust
18. rant
19. find
20. plum

4.4 Transferring letters

1. (c) at, chose
2. (r) beak, tear
3. (h) cook, hair
4. (f) lock, fair
5. (e) not, ripe
6. (t) meal, part
7. (u) lot, menu
8. (p) seed, spell
9. (h) cat, champ
10. (c) lie, scale

4.5 Practice

1. hurt
2. ever
3. lout
4. bale
5. lion
6. in, to
7. stop, watch
8. foot, print
9. sun, day
10. beet, root
11. liner
12. bleak
13. ache
14. lady
15. last
16. (u) for, unit
17. (s) tone, stag
18. (l) fare, cold or clod
19. (a) far, read
20. (c) hat, cloud

5.1 Simple Codes

1. 347227
2. REGION
3. 3257
4. 4871
5. DARE
6. NOTE
7. HBOEL
8. LEAF
9. DOOR
10. LPSME

5.2 Adding Codes

1. ANNJ
2. PLAY
3. BSVC
4. APNUM
5. DRINK
6. SSOJ
7. QQTV
8. DOOR
9. DOES
10. PKEG

5.3 Number Codes

1. 18 11 14 22
2. TALK
3. 16 25 7 12
4. 8 8 23 4
5. TOLD
6. DUST
7. 10 17 4 11
8. TIME
9. LOSE
10. 12 L 14 M

5.4 Alphabet Reflections

1. H V M W
2. WIND
3. S F I G
4. S R E V
5. EXAM
6. FALL
7. X Z O U
8. PENS
9. THIS
10. K O Z B

5.5 Practice

1. S B J O
2. THANK
3. U G L B M U
4. T J R I X
5. AIRCRAFT
6. SHARK
7. I T X W Q O
8. FIRST
9. FRIEND
10. K M T G C
11. 26 2 13 21 14
12. OUTFIT
13. 7 Q 19 G 20 V
14. RIDER
15. U 7 B 18 F
16. GRASS
17. H J F Z I V
18. TASTE
19. TAIL
20. T I V Z G

6.1 Links

1. 6
2. 2
3. 3
4. 5
5. 10
6. 5
7. 15
8. 2
9. 2
10. 4
11. 11
12. 20
13. 71
14. 9
15. 36
16. 14
17. 10
18. 30
19. 6
20. 10

6.2 Substitution

1. 4
2. 10
3. 4
4. 4
5. 8
6. D
7. C
8. A
9. C
10. E

6.3 Equalities

1. 2
2. 10
3. 4
4. 7
5. 5
6. 9
7. 3
8. 8
9. 2
10. 4

6.4 Number Sequences

1. 13
2. 10
3. 32
4. 28
5. 250
6. 4
7. 10
8. 5
9. 16
10. 6

6.5 Practice

1. 24
2. 3
3. 20
4. 4
5. 30
6. C
7. E
8. C
9. A
10. D
11. 27
12. 5
13. 1
14. 4
15. 6
16. 48
17. 15
18. 25
19. 12
20. 8

7.1 Mixed up Codes

1. 2163
2. FEAR
3. 6153
4. 7513
5. TENT
6. 36751
7. 3175
8. FARE
9. RATS
10. 4231

7.2 Go With Two Groups

1. staff
2. minute
3. rose
4. land
5. stone
6. mole
7. close
8. pound
9. book
10. flat

7.3 Word Analogies

1. second, silver
2. fresh, polluted
3. foal, cub
4. whine, deer
5. pride, school
6. right, no
7. milk, paper
8. talk, firm
9. meat, bread
10. nail, staple

7.4 Belonging

1. second
2. lungs
3. Athens
4. newsagent
5. teenager
6. electrician
7. taxi
8. whole
9. ash
10. projector

7.5 Practice

1. 9354
2. STEW
3. WINNER
4. 4745
5. HEARTH
6. 2534
7. watch
8. bear
9. nail
10. left
11. drank, found
12. ram, stag
13. lose, demolish
14. flakes, drops
15. pain, way
16. cup
17. hundred
18. double bass
19. square
20. bean

8.1 What number?

1. 40
2. 17
3. Joanna and Alison
4. 600
5. 10
6. Baljeet
7. 5
8. 7
9. 107
10. 3

8.2 What Time?

1. January
2. 8:09a.m.
3. 10:15p.m.
4. 1:00a.m.
5. 80 minutes
6. December
7. 50 minutes
8. 18:00
9. 28
10. 120 years

8.3 Can(not) be True

1. A
2. B
3. D
4. B
5. D
6. B
7. C
8. D
9. D
10. C

8.4 Sorting Info

1. Nasir
2. Hamza
3. Kane
4. D
5. Ola
6. C
7. A
8. Ryszard
9. Townville
10. 3

8.5 Practice

1. B
2. French
3. Terrence
4. Priyanka
5. Winston
6. D
7. Julian, Ida
8. 6 minutes
9. 14:42
10. D

9.1 Comprehension

1. C
2. B
3. A
4. A
5. C
6. D
7. C
8. C
9. B
10. B

9.2 Cloze

1. teacher, student, how
2. orbits, sun, year
3. seed, of, oak
4. goes, is, closed
5. sells, milk, goats
6. become, for, first
7. excited, his, weeks
8. are, become, not
9. capital, Scotland, Edinburgh
10. accident, yesterday, jam

9.3 Two Words Between

1. CARE / CORE or FARE
2. FACE / FACT
3. BENT / BEAT
4. LOST / LOSE
5. SLOT / PLOT or SLOP
6. FLAP / FLAW / FLOP
7. ROSE / ROLE
8. CHAT / COAT
9. SALE / BALE
10. GRAND / GLAND or BRAND

9.4 Extra Words

1. dream
2. drink
3. is
4. reads
5. primitive
6. was
7. the
8. stars
9. an
10. will

9.5 Practice

1. D
2. A
3. B
4. B
5. D
6. electrician, wired, sold
7. four, sides, no
8. carbon dioxide, and oxygen
9. animals, active, night
10. friction, force, opposes
11. SHOP / SHIP
12. FILL / SILL
13. ALONG / ALONE
14. SHORE / CHORE
15. STEP / STOP
16. treats
17. is
18. lots
19. moon
20. low

10.1 Crossword Grids

1.

S	H	O	R	T
T				R
A	B	O	D	E
R				A
T	Y	P	E	D

2.

F	R	O	W	N
E				O
A	D	O	P	T
S				C
T	O	U	G	H

3.

T	O	R	C	H
R				O
U	R	B	A	N
T				E
H	U	R	R	Y

4.

S	H	O	R	E
T				X
R	I	N	S	E
A				R
Y	E	A	S	T

5.

C	H	A	N	T
R				R
E	X	T	R	A
S				I
T	A	K	E	N

6.

C	L	O	V	E
A		A		D
B		S		G
I		I		E
N	O	S	E	S

7.

E	V	E	R	Y
T		L		A
H		D	E	W
O		E		N
S	O	R	T	S

8.

A	T	E
N	O	W
T	E	E

9

H	A	U	L
A	C	R	E
U	R	G	E
L	E	E	K

10.

L	E	A	S	T
A	H	I		O
K		S	O	W
E		L		E
S	P	E	A	R

10.2 Definitions

1. donation
2. rhombus
3. legible
4. gratitude
5. focus
6. slack
7. scrawl
8. errand
9. elaborate
10. current

10.3 Letters Missing

1. ACK
2. MIN
3. NESD or DNES
4. ICE
5. CRE
6. ETA
7. DUS
8. HOD
9. IMP
10. PEA

10.4 Scrabble Words

1. girl
2. tin
3. ring
4. age
5. gale
6. lie
7. live
8. bled
9. dive
10. slide

10.5 Practice

1.

S	E	A
H	A	D
E	R	A

2.

S	O	L	I	D
A				A
F	I	V	E	R
E				E
R	A	P	I	D

3.

S	A	B	R	E
T		A		M
O		S	E	A
N		I		I
E	X	C	E	L

4.

G	E	R	M	S
E		E		C
N		L	E	A
U		A		L
S	T	Y	L	E

5.

S	P	R	E	A	D
P	I	E	R	C	E
R	E	G	R	E	T
E	R	R	A	T	A
A	C	E	T	I	C
D	E	T	A	C	H

6. Will
7. Trilogy
8. Tsunami
9. Hospitable
10. Brave
11. HOPP
12. ICE
13. ESE
14. ECT
15. CAS
16. scent
17. ten
18. tense
19. fine
20. sent

11.1 Two Letters

1. ZE
2. VE
3. TH
4. ST
5. TE
6. OW
7. GE
8. AM
9. ED
10. IT

11.2 Anagrams

1. computer
2. silent
3. elephants
4. prescribed
5. limestone
6. average
7. circus
8. century
9. justify
10. tomorrow

11.3 Word in Front

1. over
2. for
3. out
4. sun
5. back
6. foot
7. pass
8. fire
9. head
10. sand

11.4 Word Structure

1. ought, tough
2. start, tarts
3. thin, hint
4. towel
5. frost
6. wasps
7. kayak
8. minim
9. rough, stuff
10. cheque, wreck

11.5 Practice

1. CH
2. CE
3. RE
4. SH
5. AN
6. rubbish
7. clouds
8. orchestra
9. listen
10. assortment
11. up
12. soft
13. hand
14. sea
15. post
16. easel, lease
17. night, thing
18. flesh, shelf
19. shrub, brush
20. racecar

12.1 Revision Set 1

1. (u) fond, could
2. (s) till, gifts
3. (f) old, fill
4. (b) eat, bold
5. (n) had, never
6. seven
7. April
8. day
9. son
10. milk
11. 8
12. 19
13. 10
14. 13
15. 25
16. narrow, thin
17. fast, quick
18. talk, speak
19. thought, idea
20. minus, subtract

12.2 Revision Set 2

1. QR, ST
2. MR, NT
3. HM, KJ
4. IN, KO
5. KS, HV
6. length, width
7. oak, acorn
8. morning, breakfast
9. meal, food
10. fib, sing
11. 18
12. 30
13. 6
14. 5
15. 20
16. YES
17. VKP
18. JHD
19. HOT
20. JMR

12.3 Revision Set 3

1. IK
2. RU
3. UT
4. UW
5. WX
6. land, mark
7. rug, by
8. but, ton
9. seed, ling
10. for, tune
11. 15
12. 10
13. 5
14. 10
15. 4
16. leaves, trees, ground
17. judge, court, yesterday
18. limit, miles, per
19. water, your, kidneys
20. won, became, king

12.4 Revision Set 4

1. land
2. fable
3. might
4. bent
5. frown
6. 2000
7. 12
8. 125
9. 30
10. 11
11. silver, cloud
12. drain, coin
13. a, all
14. in, were
15. help, has
16. AL
17. RE
18. FE
19. TE
20. AT

12.5 Revision Set 5

1. rinse
2. rein / reins
3. ruin
4. oven
5. vine
6. C
7. B
8. D
9. E
10. B
11. cellar
12. hearth
13. yearn
14. alter
15. taper
16. lead (mule, adjusted)
17. file (fulfil every)
18. call (identical, lion)
19. rash (camera, shoot)
20. barn (bar, never)

Printed in Great Britain
by Amazon

77615716R00043